The **Jewish** Experience

Jan Thompson

Foundation

Hodder & Stoughton

A MEMBER OF THE HODDER HEADLINE GROUP

Acknowledgements

Dedicated to:
Jo Daykin, a friend and colleague.

Notes:

> CE = Common Era
> BCE = Before the Common Era
>
> CE corresponds to AD, and BCE corresponds to BC. The years are the same, but CE and BCE can be used by anyone regardless of their religion. (AD and BC are Christian: AD stands for Anno Domini – in the Year of Our Lord, i.e. Jesus Christ; BC stands for Before Christ.)

Key words are explained in the glossary on page 62.

Orders: please contact Bookpoint Ltd, 39 Milton Park, Abingdon, Oxon OX14 4TD. Telephone: (44) 01235 400414, Fax: (44) 01235 400454. Lines are open from 9.00–6.00, Monday to Saturday, with a 24 hour message answering service. Email address: orders@bookpoint.co.uk

British Library Cataloguing in Publication Data
A catalogue record for this title is available from The British Library

ISBN 0 340 77585 8

First published 2000

Impression number	10	9	8	7	6	5	4	3	2	1
Year	2005	2004	2003	2002	2001	2000				

Copyright © 2000 Jan Thompson, Liz Aylett and Kevin O'Donnell

Cover photo from David Rose.
All illustrations supplied by Daedalus, with special thanks to John McIntyre.
Typeset by Wearset, Boldon, Tyne and Wear.
Printed for Hodder & Stoughton Educational, a division of Hodder Headline Plc, 338 Euston Road, London NW1 3BH by Printer Trento, Italy

The Publishers would like to thank the following for permission to reproduce material in this volume:

BBC for the quote on page 59 by Nathan Sharansky from *When I Get To Heaven*, 1987 and the quote on page 60 by Julia Neuberger from *Open Space*; BBC/The Chief Rabbi for the extract on page 44 from the broadcast by the Chief Rabbi, Radio 3, Eve of Rosh Hashanah, September 1987; Channel 4 for the quote on page 60 by Gerson Cohen from *Heritage Conversation*, January 1988; HarperCollins for the extracts on pages 15 & 30 from *This is My God* by Herman Wouk; *Jewish Chronicle* for the quotations on page 59 by Ida Nudel, reproduced by permission; Penguin UK for the extracts on page 53 from *The Diary of a Young Girl: The Definitive Edition* by Anne Frank, edited by Otto Frank and Mirjam Pressler, translated by Susan Massotty (Viking, 1997) copyright © The Anne Frank-Fonds, Basle, Switzerland, 1991. English translation copyright © Doubleday, a division of Bantam Doubleday Dell Publishing Group Inc, 1995. Reproduced by permission of Penguin Books Ltd.

Minor adaptations have been made to some quotations to render them more accessible to the readership.

The Publishers would like to thank the following for their permission to reproduce copyright photographs in this book:

AKG Photo, London: p. 53; Ancient Art and Architecture Collection Ltd: p. 16; Associated Press Library: pp. 54, 56, 32, 41, 48, 59; Hulton Getty: pp. 9, 21r; Life File: pp. 4, 14, 17, 19l; Christine Osborne/MEP: pp. 8, 18, 26l, 28, 37, 47, 50, 55, 58; David Rose: pp. 7, 26r, 27, 29, 31, 36, 42, 49; Topham Picturepoint: pp. 22, 23.

Every effort has been made to trace and acknowledge ownership of copyright. The publishers will be glad to make suitable arrangements with any copyright holders whom it has not been possible to contact.

Contents

◀ A Jewish Family

The people on these 2 pages all have one thing in common. They are Jews. You cannot tell Jews from the way they look. There are black Jews and white Jews. There are fair-haired Jews and dark-haired Jews.

Jews came from Israel in the Middle East. About 2000 years ago, they were forced to leave Israel, and they spread all over the world. In 1948 Israel was set up again as a Jewish country. Many Jews have gone back to live in Israel. But there are many more living in non-Jewish countries.

Many Jews are famous in the world of entertainment. There are famous Jewish singers and musicians. There are famous Jewish film-makers and TV stars. Some Jews are famous scientists. Some have made important discoveries in medicine.

4

▼ *Jews live in many countries in the world today*

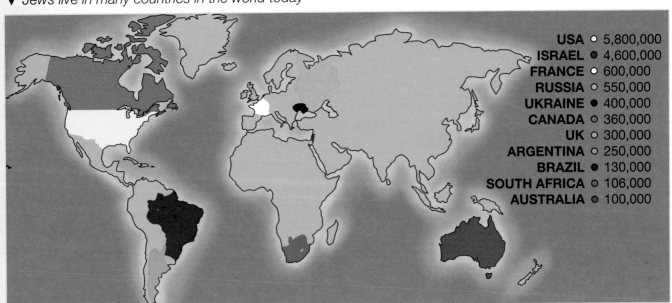

USA ○	5,800,000
ISRAEL ●	4,600,000
FRANCE ○	600,000
RUSSIA ○	550,000
UKRAINE ●	400,000
CANADA ○	360,000
UK ○	300,000
ARGENTINA ○	250,000
BRAZIL ●	130,000
SOUTH AFRICA ○	106,000
AUSTRALIA ◉	100,000

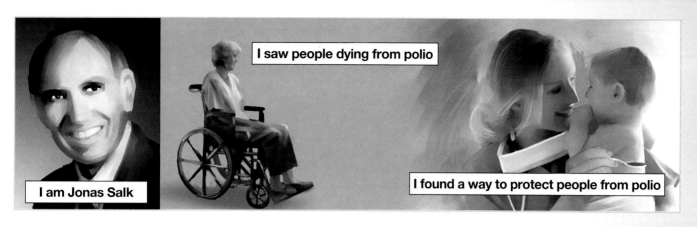

I saw people dying from polio

I am Jonas Salk

I found a way to protect people from polio

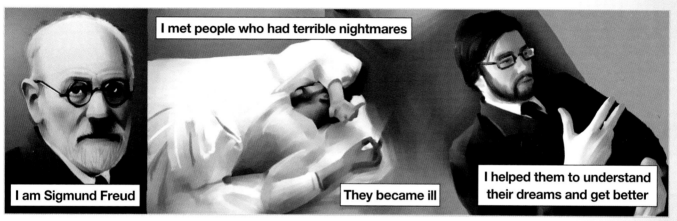

I met people who had terrible nightmares

I am Sigmund Freud

They became ill

I helped them to understand their dreams and get better

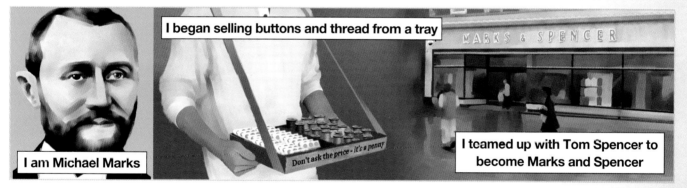

I began selling buttons and thread from a tray

MARKS & SPENCER

Don't ask the price - it's a penny

I am Michael Marks

I teamed up with Tom Spencer to become Marks and Spencer

▲ *Three famous Jews are shown in the pictures above. You may not have heard of all of them, but everyone has heard of Marks & Spencer!*

1 Ask your teacher to tell you about another famous Jew. Draw your own picture-strip about him or her. Add captions.

2 The 3 men above helped the world in different ways. In pairs, talk about who you think was most helpful. Explain why.

3 Think of a talent that you have. Under a photo or drawing of yourself, write about your talent. Is it something that will make the world a better place?

TASK

Think about how many relatives you have. Do you know them all? Or do you have some distant relatives that you have never met?
How far back can you go through your grandparents, great-grandparents, etc?

6

◀ The remains of a temple at ancient Ur

The Jewish people believe they can trace their beginnings back to a man called Abraham. They call him the Father of the Jews. He lived nearly 4000 years ago. He came from a country in the Middle East.

Abraham was born in the city of Ur. The remains of this very old city have been dug up. One of the most exciting finds is shown in the photo. It was a mound of bricks that was taller than all the other buildings in the city. On top of it there used to be a temple where people worshipped the Sun and Moon as gods.

Most people at that time worshipped many gods. But Abraham came to believe that there was only One God.

▼ The map shows the Middle East in Abraham's time. Can you find Ur, where he was born? He moved from there to Haran, when he was young

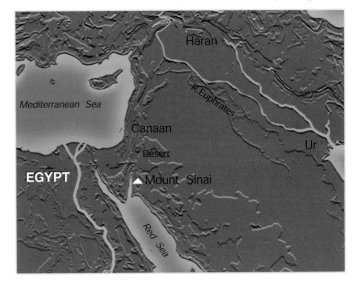

Haran
R. Euphrates
Mediterranean Sea
Canaan
Desert
Ur
EGYPT
Mount Sinai
Red Sea

The Bible tells how God told Abraham to leave his home and travel to another country. This was when he was an old man. God promised Abraham that he would be the father of a great nation. God promised him that this nation would settle in the land which was later called Israel.

Abraham was puzzled. He had no children, and he and his wife were old. But he trusted God. He packed up and left Haran for the Promised Land.

His wife Sarah had a son in her old age. They called him Isaac, which means 'laughter', because he made them so happy.

Abraham thought that God wanted him to sacrifice Isaac. There was a belief that if the first child was a boy, he belonged to God. It was a custom in those days to kill the first-born son as an offering to God. The Bible says that God stopped Abraham from doing this. Abraham sacrificed a ram instead.

The Jews never sacrificed humans, only animals. 2000 years ago, they stopped sacrificing animals also.

▼ *A statue of Abraham and the ram*

Key words

ancient
Bible
sacrifice
Abraham

1 Draw a picture of Abraham and the ram. Underneath it:

 a) Say what Abraham nearly did to his son Isaac.

 b) Explain why.

 c) What did he sacrifice instead?

2 a) What did the ancient Jews think a 'sacrifice' was?

 b) What do we mean today when we 'make a sacrifice' for someone?

 c) What would you give up for someone you love?

Abraham's children settled in the Promised Land. Many years later there was a famine there. So they moved to Egypt where there was plenty of food. At first everything went well. Later the Egyptians used them as slaves.

A great man became leader of the Jews. His name was Moses. The most important story about Moses is called the Exodus. (The word 'exodus' is a bit like 'exit'. It means 'to go out'.) Moses stood up to the Pharaoh, the ruler of Egypt. Finally, he led the Jews out of Egypt. There is a book in the Bible called Exodus. It tells the story of Moses.

The Book of Exodus describes 10 plagues that happened in Egypt. Look at each picture below and think about what happened.

1 Low water in the River Nile turned mud-red.
2 The frogs came out onto the land.
3 Maggots bred in their dead bodies.
4 Flies hatched and carried disease.
5 Animals became ill.
6 It spread to people.
7 The weather changed.
8 Locusts ate the crops.
9 The clouds of locusts darkened the sky.
10 Many died.

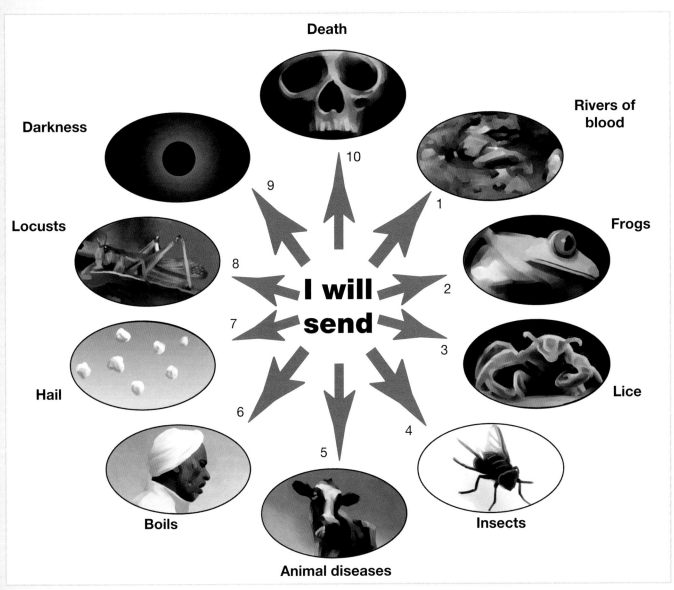

▲ *The 10 plagues*

◄ *Young African slaves*

The people believed that God sent all these things to make the Pharaoh free the Jews. In the end the Pharaoh gave in!

The story of the Exodus was told and retold every year at the festival of Passover. Why would the Jews make up a story about being slaves, unless it was true?

Thousands of years later, other slaves heard this story. When African slaves were taken to America and the West Indies, they were told stories from the Bible. They heard how God's special people had been slaves. They heard how God had helped them escape. This gave them hope. They told their own stories about Moses and sang their own songs about him. These are known as Negro spirituals. Music such as the blues and jazz came from this style.

> **Key words**
>
> **famine**
> **Moses**
> **Exodus**
> **Pharaoh**
> **plague**
> **Passover**

1 The 10 plagues were natural disasters. They were not man-made.

a) With your partner, make a list of natural disasters that can happen now. There may be one in the news at the moment.

b) Natural disasters are sometimes called 'acts of God'. Do you think that God makes these things happen? Are any of them caused by human actions?

2 Imagine you are a Jewish parent. Your 6-year-old child asks you to tell her about the Exodus. Work with a partner to decide what to tell her about –
● what happened
● its result
● what it taught the Jews about God.

◀ *Pharaoh's dream from the musical,* Joseph and the Amazing Technicolour Dream Coat. *Ask your teacher to tell you the story of Joseph*

● The Tenach

The Bible is the holy book of the Jews. They call it the Tenach. It is a very old collection of writings, in 3 parts:
- Torah (teachings)
- Prophets
- Writings (songs and sayings).

Jews have other holy books to help them understand the Bible.

The Jewish Bible has many different things in it. It has the history of the Jews. There are poems and wise sayings. And there are lots of different kinds of stories.

Many Bible stories are well known. Some have been made into films or musicals.

Linking all these things together is the idea that God loved and guided the Jews through the ages. Again and again, he has saved them from their enemies. The Bible teaches the Jews about God. It teaches them how he wants them to live.

The Jewish Bible is important to Christians too. It is the Christian Old Testament – the first part of the Christian Bible.

1 a) Draw and label a diagram to remind you of the 3 parts of the Jewish Bible. Leave space above and below the picture.

b) Make a list of FOUR different things you can find in the Bible. Write these words above your picture.

c) Make a list of THREE things Jews can learn from the Bible about God. Write these below your picture.

The Torah

We all have our own rules that we try to live by. It might be to treat others as you would like them to treat you. This is a rule for living. You may have a particular care for animals or the environment. All of these things are our rules for living.

The first 5 books of the Jewish Bible are called the Torah. This word means 'teachings'. The Torah is a mixture of stories and laws. It has stories about the creation of the world. It gives the early history of the Jews, ending with the death of Moses. It contains 316 rules for the Jews to live by.

These many rules are summed up in the Ten Commandments. The Bible says that God gave these 10 laws to the Jews after they had run away from Egypt. Moses went to meet God at the top of Mount Sinai. He came down with 2 slabs of stone. The Ten Commandments were written on them.

So the Jewish way of life is given to them in their Bible. Jews love God and want to please him. This is why they try to keep his commandments.

▲ *What are this person's rules for living?   What things does she care about?*

Key words

Tenach
rabbi
Torah
commandment

▼ *Moses brought the Jews the Ten Commandments*

Some of the rules in the Torah no longer apply. There are many rules about temple sacrifices. But the Jews no longer have a temple. Nor do they offer sacrifices.

> The commandments in the Torah are my guide to living.
>
> The people in the Torah are real people that I can identify with.
>
> I firmly believe in the Torah as a complete way of life. I don't consider it to be a holy way of life. It is simply my way of life.

For the Jewish woman who said this, the Torah is much more than a book – it has rules which teach Jews what they should do in just about every part of their lives.

● Prophets

Many books in the Bible are about the prophets. The Jews believe that the prophets brought messages from God. Sometimes they prophesied about the future. But mostly they spoke out against the evils of their own times. They even spoke out against the kings!

▲ *How many of the Ten Commandments can you see in these pictures?*

The Ten Commandments:

1 I am the Lord your God
2 You must have no other gods but me
3 You must not misuse God's name
4 Keep the Sabbath day holy
5 Respect your father and mother
6 Do not murder
7 Do not commit adultery
8 Do not steal
9 Do not give false evidence
10 Do not envy other people.

1 The last 5 commandments begin with 'Do not'. Rewrite each one so that it starts with 'Always'. For example, number 8 could be 'Always leave other people's things alone.'

2 Choose the commandment that you think is most important. Discuss this with your partner and explain your reasons.

3 Think about your own rules for living:
   a) What rules do you try to live by?
   b) Where did you get these rules from (eg parents, school, friends, club . . .)?

Elijah

One great prophet was called Elijah. The king at the time had let his wife bring her religion to Israel with her. Its priests worshipped idols. Elijah challenged them to a contest, to prove which was the true god. They each built an altar. They prayed to their gods to send fire from heaven to burn up their sacrifices. The others prayed and prayed. But nothing happened. Then Elijah prayed to the One God: 'O Lord, God of Abraham ... let it be known today that you are God in Israel!' At that moment, lightning struck the altar and burnt it up. It was the beginning of a storm, and the first rain for several years.

There are many other stories about Elijah. One of them tells how he was taken up to heaven in a chariot of fire. Jews believe that Elijah will return to earth one day. A place is set at table for him every year at the celebration of the Passover!

Nathan

Another prophet was called Nathan. He was so brave that he stood up to King David. David was the greatest king of the Jews. David had an affair with a married woman when her husband was away fighting in his army. When the woman became pregnant, David got rid of her husband so that he could marry her himself. He gave orders for her husband to be put in the front line of the battle, and he was killed. The prophet Nathan told King David a story which made him realise he had done wrong.

13

▲ *The prophet Nathan visits King David*

● Songs and Sayings

A well-known part of the Bible is the Book of Psalms (don't pronounce the 'p'). They are religious poems, or songs. King David was a musician, and he is said to have written the Psalms. They were probably written by other people as well. Whoever wrote them, they were very honest and open about their feelings:

> My God, my God, why have you forsaken me?
> Why are you so far from helping me
> O my God, I cry by day, but you do not
> answer; and by night, but find no rest.

Other Psalms are full of faith in God, such as Psalm 23:

> The Lord is my shepherd, I shall not want.
> He makes me lie down in green pastures;
> he leads me beside still waters;
> he restores my soul . . .

Another well-known part of the Bible is the Book of Proverbs. Proverbs are wise sayings.

Key words

prophet
psalm
proverb

- ● Wine is a mocker, strong drink a brawler, and whoever is led astray by it is not wise.

- ● It is honourable to refrain from strife, but every fool is quick to quarrel.

- ● A soft answer turns away wrath, but a harsh word stirs up anger.

- ● Happy are those who find wisdom, and those who get understanding, for her income is better than silver, and her revenue better than gold.

1 Ask your teacher to tell you THREE wise sayings. Talk about their meanings

2 Psalm 23 is the best-known Psalm. Ask your teacher to read it out in full, while you look at the photo on this page. Choose your favourite line from Psalm 23. Write it out under a picture that you have drawn or stuck into your book.

14

▶ *Beside still waters*

One God

> **TASK**
>
> Few people in Britain practise any religion. But most people still believe in God. Do a survey in your class. It should be anonymous. Find out how many of you a) believe in God, and b) believe in life after death.

Jews believe that there is only One God. They believe he created the world and that he sees and knows everything.

▼ *The Shema*

שְׁמַ֖ע יִשְׂרָאֵ֑ל
יְהוָ֥ה אֱלֹהֵ֖ינוּ
יְהוָ֥ה ׀ אֶחָֽד׃

Shema Yisrael, Adonai Elohenu, Adonai Echad.
Hear, O Israel, the Lord our God, the Lord is one.

The first Hebrew a Jewish child learns is the Shema (pronounced sh-maa). It is from the Torah. It is written out here in Hebrew and English. Notice that the first word is 'Shema'. (Ask your teacher to try to read what it sounds like in Hebrew.)

The Shema should also be the last thing a Jew says before death. The American playwright, Herman Wouk, tells us about it:

> I used to wonder if a man could really remember the Shema when he was dying. Then once, during a storm in the Pacific, I was almost blown off the deck of a ship. I remember clearly thinking, as I slid down, 'Well, if I drown, let me say the Shema as I go.'

Jews believe that God watches over the world and cares for all the people in it. Jews try to follow God's example. One way is not to do anything to others that you wouldn't want done to you. This is called the Golden Rule. The Torah says:

> Do not get your own back on anyone or continue to hate him, but love your neighbour as you love yourself.

▲ *Young Jewish children learning the Shema*

15

● The Messiah

The idea of the Messiah comes from the Bible. The word means 'anointed one'. The kings of old were anointed with oil when they were made king. So the Bible looked forward to a new king of the Jews. He would be greater even than King David.

The followers of Jesus thought that he was the Messiah. They called him King of the Jews, and Son of David. But Jews do not agree. They are still waiting for the Messiah. This is the main difference between Jews and Christians.

Jews have different ideas about the Messiah. Some are waiting for a person to be sent from God who will make everything right on earth. Others are waiting for a new age of love and peace. Many Jews pray daily for the Messiah to come. But all Jews can work towards a world of goodness and peace.

All through history, people have claimed to be the Messiah – men of peace, like Jesus, and men of war who have led the Jews against their enemies. This picture shows a Turkish Jew who claimed to be the Messiah only 300 years ago.

▲ *Shabbetai Zevi in 1666*

The Shema

1 a) What does the Shema say about God?
b) What language is it written in?

2 Surveys show that most people in Britain believe in God. Yet only a small number of people practise a religion. If people believe in God, discuss how you think it should affect their lives.

The Golden Rule

3 Write out the Golden Rule from page 15. In pairs, work out a role-play of a situation where you can show the Golden Rule in action.

The Messiah

4 a) What do Jews believe the world will be like after the Messiah comes?
b) Discuss what you would like to change about the world.
c) Make a class collage of your ideas about a new world.

● The World to Come

The Bible teaches the Jews how they should live this life. They should not worry too much about the next.

But they do believe in life after death. The end of life on earth does not mean the end of everything. They believe that there will be another kind of life that lasts forever.

A Jewish girl tells us why she believes this:

> I believe that there is a Heaven. I think that once we die, we do go to Heaven. After reading the Torah it is obvious that G_d loves us too much to end our lives after we die.

Notice that she does not write all the letters in the word 'God'. Jews believe that God's name is holy. So they must treat it with respect. Some Jews do not like to write out the whole word. They feel it would insult God if the paper with his name on was torn or dropped.

In this book we will write the word 'God' in full. This is a school book, not a religious book. It is not written specially for Jewish pupils. But remember that any Jewish pupils among you would like God's name to be treated carefully.

◄ *Light behind dark clouds can remind people of life after death. If you believe in life after death, then it is like the sunrise after the dark clouds of death.*

Key words

Shema
Hebrew
Messiah

1 This photo can be a symbol of life after death. Can you think of other things to symbolise life after death? (Think of things where good follows bad, or where life comes out of death.) Draw your symbol.

2 Discuss in class if you believe in life after death. Give reasons for your ideas.

▲ *Inside an Orthodox synagogue*
At the front, you can see the reading desk.   Against the wall behind it is the cupboard (the Ark) for the Torah scrolls.   You can see the balconies where women and children sit.   The men sit below.

(NB synagogue is pronounced 'sin-a-gog'.)
There are 2 types of Judaism:
Orthodox Judaism is traditional – it carries on the old customs.
Reform Judaism is more modern.

The synagogue is where Jews meet together for:
● **prayer**   ● **study**   ● **talking.**
A synagogue can be large or small, old or modern.   It may be anywhere in the world.

The main synagogue services are held on the Sabbath day.   This is the Jewish holy day.   It starts on Friday evening with a service.   The family service is on Saturday morning.   Men and women sit apart in an Orthodox synagogue.   But they sit together in a Reform synagogue.

The service is read from a prayer book. Most synagogues have a rabbi to lead the service.   This is always a man in an Orthodox synagogue.   There are some women rabbis in Reform synagogues.   An Orthodox rabbi describes what happens:

We have readings from the Psalms.   We have special prayers and a reading from the Torah.   During the morning service we go up, take out one of the Torah scrolls, and take it up to the reader's desk.   Then I will open up the scroll and read from it in Hebrew.

At the end I hold up the scroll, and say a prayer in English for the Queen followed by a prayer for the State of Israel.   Then we take the scroll down again and put it back into the Ark where it is kept.   The Ark is closed.

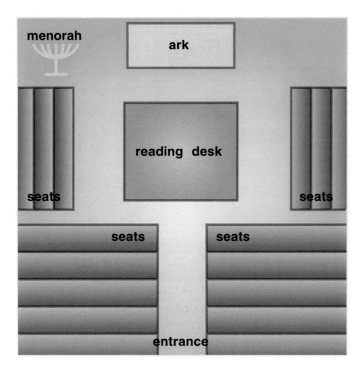

▲ *Plan of an Orthodox synagogue*

Key words

synagogue	menorah	Ark
Reform	Sabbath	Torah
Orthodox	symbol	scrolls

▲ *Lighting the menorah. This one has 8 candles and is used at a special Jewish festival*

The 7–branched candlestick (the menorah) is a symbol of Judaism. It used to stand in the Temple in Jerusalem. Synagogues often have a menorah in them.

The light of the candles reminds worshippers that God is there. The number is a holy number in Judaism. It also reminds them of the story in the Bible which says that God made the world in 7 days.

Synagogues have lots of things in them which are special to Jews. We all have our own special things. They may not be religious. But they mean a lot to us.

▲ *Do you have special things in your bedroom?*

1 Think about something which is special to you. Describe it to your partner, and explain why it is special to you.

2 Put the title: 'An Orthodox synagogue'. Copy the plan into your book. Copy out and finish these sentences:

   a) The Ark is where ...

   b) The reading desk is where ...

   c) The ground-floor seats are where ...

   d) The seats in the balcony are where ...

- In an Orthodox synagogue, nearly all the service is in Hebrew (the Jewish language). Only the prayer for the Royal Family and the talk are in English.
- In a Reform synagogue, there is more English. A Reform rabbi explains:

> There is some English in our service. The main parts of the service, such as the Shema, would nearly always be in Hebrew. In my service, I try to have something like 75 per cent Hebrew, 25 per cent English.

Some synagogues open for daily prayers. Jewish men should pray 3 times a day. But many are too busy working to go to the synagogue. This doesn't matter. They can pray anywhere.

Prayer is talking to God. There are 5 kinds of Jewish prayer:
1 To praise God
2 To ask him to care for people in need
3 To thank him for looking after everyone
4 To ask him to forgive them for doing wrong
5 To pray for peace in the world.

The most important part of the synagogue is the Ark. This is because the Torah scrolls are kept here. The most important part of the service is when the Torah is read. Jews believe that God speaks to them in the Torah. He teaches them how to live.

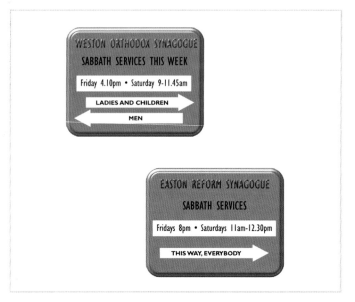

▲ *Differences between the Orthodox and Reform synagogues. The Sabbath Day starts at sunset for Orthodox Jews and 6pm for Reform Jews*

▲ *A synagogue. Notice the Hebrew writing on the wall*

1 Divide your page into TWO columns. Put the titles: 'Orthodox, Reform'. Copy these statements in the correct columns. NB Some will go in both columns! (You will need to look back at page 18.)
- I worship One God
- My synagogue allows women rabbis
- Most of the service is in Hebrew
- I sit with my husband
- The Sabbath day starts at 6pm
- The Sabbath morning service lasts several hours.

▲ *Young Jews today*

▲ *Jews about 100 years ago*

> **TASK**
>
> These 2 photos show a group of young Jews today, and a group of Jews about a hundred years ago. Many things have changed!
> * What changes can you see in the photos?

Judaism is a very old religion. Abraham, the Father of the Jews, lived almost 4000 years ago! The Jewish Bible was finished almost 2000 years ago. And much of it was written a 1000 years before that. Jews have a hard choice to make. How much of their old religion should they keep? How much should change with modern times?

Some old laws of Judaism may have been good in their time. But do they make sense now? The food laws are a good example. The Torah says that Jews must not eat pork or shellfish.

* Orthodox Jews think that this is still important. It is still a command from God.
* Some Reform Jews think it is outdated. When the law was made, people often got food poisoning from pork and shellfish. This food went off quickly in hot weather. But now we have fridges and freezers.
* Most Jews feel that the food laws are good because they set the Jews apart from other people. It helps Jews to remember their religion. It will help Judaism to go on.

1 Choose either 'Orthodox' or 'Reform' to complete these sentences. Then copy them.

a) _____Jews want to keep all the old laws. They believe they are still God's commands.

b) _____ Jews think that some of the old laws no longer make sense in the modern world.

▲ *Men and women worship together in a Reform synagogue*

One big difference between Orthodox and Reform Jews is how they treat men and women.

In the last chapter, we saw that women sit apart from the men in the synagogue. Often this is in a balcony. In a modern building, it may be in a separate block of seating. This custom goes back to the time of the Temple in Jerusalem where they had separate courtyards for men and women. The reason is that men's minds could wander from their worship of God, if they mix with women during worship! Also, the seating in an Orthodox synagogue lets the men lead the service easily. The women take no public part in the service. So they can sit in the balcony with the children, and follow the service from there.

An Orthodox Jew tells us:

> We do have different laws for men and women in Orthodox Judaism. But it doesn't mean that we're not equal. We're just different. The men have more laws to do with the synagogue. The women have more laws to do with the home.

There are many ways in which Orthodox and Reform Jews are different. But it is what they have in common that is most important. All Jews believe in the One God, and they try to live good lives.

Discuss the following questions:

1 (If there are boys and girls at your school.)

a) In what ways are girls and boys treated differently at your school? For example, think about uniform, changing-rooms, subjects, etc.

b) Do you think there are good reasons for this?

2 a) In what ways are men and women still treated differently in our society?

b) Do you think there are good reasons for this?

3 Orthodox Jews say that men play an important part in the synagogue, and women play an important part in the home. Do you think this is fair?

TASK

Many people are happy to tell others what they support. A football fan wears the strip and scarf. At election time, you will see lots of posters in people's windows.

● What other kinds of posters do people put in their windows?

People stick posters in their windows to tell us what they believe in. In the same way, you can tell a Jewish home by its front door. If you look carefully, you will see a little box nailed to the door-frame. It is called a mezuzah. Inside the box is a tiny scroll with these words: 'Hear O Israel, the Lord Our God, the Lord is One . . .'

These words come from the Bible and they sum up Jewish beliefs. They are called the Shema (see page 15). The Bible tells Jews to write these words on their doorposts. And that is exactly what they do. As they go into their house, they touch the mezuzah. It reminds them that God is there with them. It reminds them to keep the Jewish rules in their home.

▼ *This mezuzah has a Jewish symbol on the top and bottom. They are the Star of David and the Menorah In the middle is the first letter of the Hebrew word for Almighty. This is a name for God*

23

▲ *A mezuzah is being fixed in place*

Family life is very important for Jews. They have many customs in the home which only Jewish people do – like touching the mezuzah. This keeps the Jewish family together. It has also helped Judaism to survive. These customs remind Jews of their beliefs. This is particularly important for Jews who live among non-Jews. They could easily adopt the ways of those around them.

> If we as Jews have survived as a people . . . it is because we've had stable homes. We grew up in places where happiness made up for many of the problems outside.
>
> *Chief Rabbi*

Key word

mezuzah

▲ *What would you put on your bedroom door frame instead of a mezuzah? Would it be a CD cover, like the boy in the picture? Would it be a photo? Would it be something special you have been given? Talk about it with your friends.*

1 a) What is a mezuzah?

   b) What does it remind Jews about?

2 Make a mezuzah. Find a small box that you can decorate. Make up your own design. Write the 'Hear O Israel . . .' on a piece of paper to go inside.

TASK

Work with a partner.

- Make a list of FIVE things which make a happy family
- Share your ideas as a class and decide on the top THREE.

In Jewish homes, the children learn to be good Jews.

The Jewish father must:

- support his family
- study the Torah
- see that his children study the Torah.

The Jewish mother must:

- follow Jewish rules when feeding the family
- make sure her husband and sons have the right clothes
- get the home ready for the Sabbath Day and other festivals
- teach her daughters how to run a Jewish home.

In many Jewish homes these jobs are now shared. But the mother is still very important. She is often the one who sees that Jewish customs are kept in the home. She brings up the children to be Jewish. Here is what 2 Jewish mothers have to say about it:

- The home is the most important place in the Jewish religion. The home is where the children are brought up and educated. It is where the festivals take place. The woman is called 'the foundation of the home'. I would say she is the most important thing in Judaism.

- Having children has made me more aware of my religion . . . I have to make sure my home backs up the things they learn at their Jewish school.

---

1 Talk in class about what it means to call the mother 'the foundation of the home'.

2 Make a list of the most important things *your* mother does?

3 Do you think a man could do all these things just as well as a woman? Talk about it with your partner.

● Food

▲ *A Jewish food shop. All the food it sells is kosher*

Food which fulfils Jewish rules is called kosher. This means that it is 'fit' for Jews to eat. Jews buy their food at kosher food shops and restaurants. At home, the mother must know all about the Jewish food laws.

Jews show their love for God by keeping the rules he has given them.

Key word
kosher

TASK

What food rules do you have? Think why you have them. For example:

● Do you wash your hands before cooking and eating?
● Are there some foods you would never eat (like eels, or horsemeat)?

Make a list of all the food rules that the class has. See how many you can think of!

26

Jews have lots of food laws too. They come from the Bible. Here are some of them:

● They must not eat anything that comes from the pig, eg pork, bacon and ham.
● They must not eat shellfish or any sea animal without fins and scales.
● They must not eat meat with blood still in it.
● They must not eat meat and milky foods in the same meal.

A Jewish kitchen has two of everything: one fridge for meat and one for milk; one set of pans for meat and one for milk; one set of plates for meat and one for milky foods; one lot of cutlery for meat and one for milk; and two sinks to wash them up.

Reform Jews may not be quite so strict about this as Orthodox Jews.

▲ *Preparing kosher food*

1 Read Deuteronomy 14: 3–21.
Make TWO columns on a page. Head one column *yes* for permitted foods and the other *no* for foods which are not allowed. Then put these foods in the correct column: lamb chops; prawn-flavoured crisps; pork sausages; chicken curry and rice; cod and chips; ham and mushroom pizza; roast beef and Yorkshire pudding.

2 In groups, plan a 3-course meal for an Orthodox Jewish family. You may have as many vegetables and fruit as you wish.

● Clothes

Most Jewish teenagers wear what they want out of school. Or they wear what their parents will buy them! But **there are special clothes for prayer**. Once a boy is over 13, he and the men wear the 3 things shown in the picture below.

   The boy may have woken up thinking about the film he saw last night, or the homework he forgot to do. But while putting on these clothes for prayer, he will have time to bring his mind back to God.

Skull cap (kippa)

'My children wear their kippa whenever we're doing anything religious.'

Prayer boxes (tefillin)

These 2 boxes have the Shema written inside them (like the mezuzah). The Bible says, 'Tie them on your arms and wear them on your foreheads as a reminder.'

Prayer shawl (tallit)

This is to remind them that God is all around them.

1 Write a sentence about each of the words in the word box. Show that you know what they mean.

2 Draw a simple sketch of the boy in the photo above. Label the THREE things he wears for prayer.

3 Do you have any clothes that you have to wear on special occasions?

There is an old saying: 'All work and no play makes Jack a dull boy!' We all need to rest and play, as well as work. That is why we look forward to the weekends when we have more time to do what we want. Have you ever wondered where the 7-day week came from? Have you ever wondered who first started weekends?

There is a very old story in the Bible that tells how God made the world. You can find this story in the very first chapter of the Bible. The story is in 7 parts. It tells how God made the world in 6 days. He rested on the 7th day.

So we know that, 2500 years ago, the Jews had a 7-day week. And we know that they had a day off each week. The story says: 'God blessed the 7th day and made it holy.

The Jews still keep the 7th day special. It is a Sabbath day because they 'stop' their normal work. This is what 'Sabbath' means. The Hebrew for 'Sabbath' is 'Shabbat'.

▲ *We all need to rest and play*

▲ *Jews eat 2 special loaves on Shabbat. They are called challot (the 'ch' sounds like a hard 'h').*

1 Write out a timetable for a normal week. Your teacher could give you a blank form to fill in. Use THREE different colours to show: (i) work (ii) rest and (iii) play.

2 If possible, your teacher will buy a challah loaf from a supermarket. (The name 'challah' is the singular of 'challot', in Hebrew.) Notice what it looks and tastes like.

◄ *If you look carefully, you can see the 2 plaited loaves. The family is sharing bread and wine*

Shabbat starts on Friday evening (because all Jewish days start in the evening). There is lots to do beforehand. The house is cleaned. Everyone is washed and well dressed. The table is laid specially and a lovely meal is prepared. All this has to be done before Shabbat. No work can be done once it has started.

The mother lights some candles to show that Shabbat has begun. There must be at least 2 candles. She says a prayer as she does it. One Jewish mother tells us what happens in her Jewish home:

> The girls light their own candles. It makes them an important part of the home.
>
> Candlelight is different from electric light. It reminds us that peace comes into the house at Shabbat.

The father and boys come back from synagogue. They all wish each other 'Shabbat Shalom' – 'A Happy Sabbath'. The father prays for his children and his wife.

They thank God for bread and wine, and they share it together (see the photo). Then they enjoy the Shabbat meal.

> Our family looks forward to Shabbat. It is a time when we are all together. We get together on Friday night and have a large meal. We all enjoy this very much. Shabbat is when the fast pace of the week slows down. We all relax and enjoy ourselves.

Shabbat ends on Saturday night. Wine is shared. A candle is lit. A spice box is passed round. Jews hope that all these lovely things will last them for the next week.

Key words

Shabbat
Shabbat Shalom
challah

1 Complete each of these sentences with their correct endings:

a) Sabbath begins	lights candles
b) The mother	are shared
c) The father	on Friday evening
d) All meals are	goes to synagogue
e) Bread and wine	'Shabbat Shalom'
f) Jews say	prepared beforehand

No work on the Sabbath – unless it saves lives

Shabbat has 3 purposes:
- It is a holy day when Jews worship God at synagogue.
- It is a day of rest when Jews stop their normal work.
- It is a day to spend together as a family.

Leaving the gloomy theatre where I work, I come home . . . My wife and my boys are waiting for me. They are dressed in their best clothes. We sit down to a splendid dinner. My wife and I talk about the week. The boys know that Shabbat is for asking questions. The Bible, the books and the atlas are piled up on the table.

Herman Wouk

1 Which words in this list would you use to describe Shabbat? Talk about them with your partner: happy, sad, calm, relaxed, frantic, special, noisy, enjoyable.
2 What else have you learnt about Shabbat from Herman Wouk (in the box opposite)?
3 If you had a special day each week, what would it be like? Think about these questions:
- What would be the main purpose of it?
- Who would you spend it with?
- What would you do?

● Naming and Circumcision

▲ *Parents bring their baby to synagogue.   There are different customs for boys and girls.*

A baby is born!   People want to celebrate. Parents choose the baby's name.

Most religions have a special ceremony for a new-born baby.   **In Judaism, baby boys are circumcised when they are 8 days old.** This means that the foreskin of their penis is snipped off.   This is a very old custom.   It is a sign that they are Jewish.

A baby boy is given his Hebrew name at his circumcision.   It may be different from the name on his birth certificate, the name he is called most of the time.   It is his religious name.   It is the name that links him with Judaism.   One Jewish mother explains:

> I felt part of a very big family when my children were given their Hebrew names. Our children were named in memory of dead relatives, so that they live on in our children.

Boy babies are circumcised because God gave this command to Abraham:

> Every male among you who is 8 days old must be circumcised.
>
> *Genesis 17 verse 12*

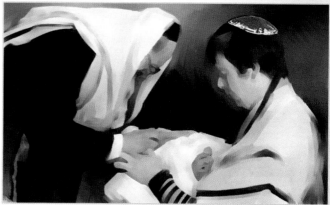

▲ *The ceremony of circumcision*

● Childhood

Jewish children can go to special classes where they learn about their religion. These often take place on a Sunday. Children can go from the age of 3.

> Judaism speaks of 4 kinds of pupils:
> **1** The sponge – he soaks up everything he learns.
> **2** The funnel – it goes in one ear and out the other.
> **3** The sifter – he remembers unimportant things and forgets the rest.
> **4** The sieve – he sorts out what is important and remembers it.

▲ *A Jewish lesson*

At religious classes, children study:
● Jewish history from the time of Abraham
● Jewish customs and ways of worship
● Hebrew, the Jewish language.

Hebrew is the old language of the Jews. The Jewish Bible is still in Hebrew. It is used in the synagogue. It is spoken today in Israel. But Jews who live outside Israel have to learn it as a second language. One Jewish girl explains what it meant to her:

> I must have been about 6 or 7 when I could read a little bit of Hebrew. I felt thrilled. I think it is important to read Hebrew if you are Jewish. God's book is written in Hebrew.

Letter	Pronunciation	Book Print
Aleph	Silent letter	א
Bet	*b* as in *boy*	בּ
	v as in *vine*	ב
Gimmel	*g* as in *girl*	ג
Dalet	*d* as in *door*	ד
Heh	*h* as in *house*	ה
Vav	*v* as in *vine*	ו
Zayin	*z* as in *zebra*	ז
Chet	*ch* as in *Bach*	ח
Tet	*t* as in *tall*	ט
Yod	*y* as in *yes*	י
Kaf	*k* as in *kitty*	כּ
	ch as in *Bach*	כ
Lamed	*l* as in *look*	ל
Mem	*m* as in *mother*	מ
Nun	*n* as in *now*	נ
Sameh	*s* as in *sun*	ס
Ayin	Silent letter	ע
Pey	*p* as in *people*	פּ
	f as in *food*	פ
Tsade	*ts* as in *nuts*	צ
Qof	*k* as in *kitty*	ק
Resh	*r* as in *robin*	ר
Shin	*sh* as in *shape*	שׁ
	s as in *sin*	שׂ
Tav	*t* as in *tall*	ת

▲ *The Hebrew alpha-bet*

● Bat and Bar Mitzvah

Jewish boys and girls have a special birthday soon after they start secondary school. When a girl is 12, she becomes Bat Mitzvah. When a boy is 13, he becomes Bar Mitzvah. This means Son or Daughter of the Commandments. They are now old enough to keep the rules of Judaism.

Reform synagogues have special services for both the girl and the boy. Orthodox synagogues only have a service for the boy. This is because only men lead their worship. At the service, the Bar Mitzvah boy reads from the Bible for the first time. He has to practise hard for this because it is in Hebrew.

> Now I have taken my Bar Mitzvah, I will wear the prayer shawl and prayer-boxes, and say the Hebrew prayers over bread and wine.

▲ *Both boys and girls may read in Reform synagogues. A boy has other duties too*

Growing up

1 What do families do to celebrate a birth?

2 How was your name chosen? Try to find out what it means.

3 What things are you allowed to do now, that you could not do when you were still at primary school?

4 When do you think children are old enough to take responsibility for their actions?

Growing up in Judaism

1 How old is a Jewish baby boy when he is circumcised?

2 What is the language of Judaism? Children are given a name in this language.

3 Why is 12 an important age for a Jewish girl?

4 What does a Jewish boy do at his Bar Mitzvah service?

◄ *A mixed race wedding. (This means that the man and woman are from different races.)*

TASK

How important is it that a married couple agree on the following? As a whole class, talk about each thing:

- money
- children
- clothes
- beliefs
- holidays
- work
- music
- background.

Then write each on a separate bit of paper. With a partner, put them in order of importance. Compare your answers with the rest of the class.

A wedding is a very happy event. People who marry are usually in love. But other things matter too. You have talked about some of these.

People who marry from different races have extra problems. And also people from different religions. If they really care for each other, it can work, but it is not always easy. A Jew explains why it is a lot easier if Jews marry Jews.

> Judaism isn't just about beliefs. It is a whole way of life. It affects the food we eat and the festivals we keep.

Most Jewish parents want their children to marry other Jews. They know that it will be much easier for them if they do. They will also pass on their religion to their children.

1 Explain why Jews usually marry other Jews.

2 Do you think it is important for a married couple to have the same religion? Explain your answer.

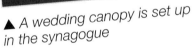
▲ A wedding canopy is set up in the synagogue

▲ The groom stamps on a wine glass!

There are many symbols at a Jewish wedding:

● **The canopy**
The bride joins the groom under a special canopy. You can see one in the photo above. It reminds them of their future home together. It shows that the groom will provide a home for his wife and any children they have.

● **The goblet**
They drink wine from the same goblet. Wine is a symbol of joy. It shows that they are going to share their lives together, in happiness.

● **The ring**
The groom puts a ring on the bride's finger. He says in Hebrew: 'You are now married to me, with this ring, by the Law of Moses and Israel.' She is now his wife.

● **The marriage contract**
This is usually a beautiful certificate. It is read out by the rabbi. In it, the groom promises to take care of his wife.

● **The 7 blessings**
The rabbi says 7 blessings over the couple. He ends by praising God 'who has created joy and gladness, bridegroom and bride, love and brotherhood, pleasure and delight, peace and harmony!'

● **Breaking of the glass**
Finally, the groom breaks a glass on the floor with his heel. You can see this in the photo above. This is a reminder that there will be bad times as well as good times ahead of them. They will face them together.

● **'Good Luck'**
At the end, everyone shouts 'Mazel Tov', which means 'Good Luck'. The service is over. Now they all look forward to joining the newly-weds at the wedding party.

▲ *A cemetery with Jewish tombstones*

The last stage in life is death. Jewish burials take place as quickly as possible. (This is because Judaism comes from Israel. Dead bodies decay quickly in hot countries.)

All are equal in death, so the service is the same for everyone. The coffin is plain and there are usually no flowers. Orthodox Jews are always buried, but Reform synagogues allow cremations.

In Orthodox Jewish families, close relatives make a small rip in their clothes to show their sadness. It is as if the death has made a rip in their lives. The family of the dead person is expected to spend the next week at home. They are encouraged to talk about how they feel. Friends bring food for them, so they do not need to cook. The men do not shave. The women do not wear make-up. They may sit on low stools and wear slippers. This is because their normal life has been interrupted by the death.

Every year, on the anniversary of the death of a parent, the children light a candle that burns for 24 hours. They say a special prayer. It is perhaps surprising that this prayer does not mention the dead person. Instead, it praises God and asks for peace:

> Blessed, praised and glorified be the Name of the Holy One, blessed be He. He who makes peace in His high places, may He make peace for us and for all Israel, and say Amen.

1 Jews take time out from work, to talk about the death of someone close to them. Do you think it is better to talk about something you feel very sad about, or to keep it to yourself? Give your reasons.

2 If you want, share with the class about a time when someone close to you died. How did you feel? How did the family react? What did you do?

3 Make up a new ritual which could be used at either a wedding or a funeral.

A minister in a synagogue is called a rabbi. This means 'my teacher.' A rabbi's main work is to teach his or her congregation to understand Judaism, and to answer their questions. Most rabbis are men, but there are some women rabbis in Reform Judaism.

A reform rabbi describes his work

- **The rabbi's job is very largely teaching**. I spend many hours teaching – both adults and children. But it goes further than that. You also teach through your example.
- **The rabbi also has a duty to care for people**. Visiting people in hospital is part of my work. Jewish people who are sick should have a visit from the rabbi. People who have got some difficulty should feel that they can turn to the rabbi for help.
- **The rabbi teaches people about Jewish rules.** There may be Jewish patients in hospital. The nurses want to do the right thing about what they eat. If they die, the nurses may be very frightened of breaking Jewish laws. So I advise them.
- **The rabbi is an ambassador to the outside world.** It is important to go to schools, for example, to talk about Judaism.
- **The rabbi is responsible for Jewish rituals.** If the wrong thing is done in a service, it is the rabbi's fault.
- **The rabbi should make sure that people feel they are useful.** For example, most of the members of staff at my synagogue are volunteers.

An orthodox rabbi describes his work

My parish work is basically the same as any other minister. I visit the sick, bury the dead, marry those who wish to be married.

I go to the local jail to visit the Jewish prisoners there. There is also a place for children with learning difficulties. I go there to tell them about God.

If people have problems that they want to share, I will listen to them. I can try to guide them along the right path, as far as possible.

I am not God's policeman. It's not my job to chase people up. I myself try to keep everything very strictly, and I like to think my congregation does too.

A rabbi takes a scroll out of the Ark ▶

A DAY IN THE LIFE OF A REFORM RABBI

TISHRI 22 5760 — OCTOBER 15 1999

9.00 Make phone calls.

10.30 Appointment with authoress.

12.30 To cemetery - check lettering on headstone.

2.00 See Mr Barnet about conversion to Judaism.

3.00 Visit Mrs Morris in hospital.

4.30 Bar Mitzvah class.

6.30 Visit another synagogue.

10.00 Time for prayer.

1 Using pages 37 and 38, list TEN things a rabbi does.

2 What kind of person do you think a rabbi should be? Talk about this list with a partner: hard-working, a good listener, tells people off, intelligent, thoughtful, likes to keep to himself or herself, kind, a good example to others. Which do you agree with and why?

3 In groups, make up an advertisement to put in a newspaper for a rabbi of a Reform synagogue. Choose a title and say what kind of person you want to apply for the job.

4 You have thought about Jewish teachers (rabbis) in this chapter. Now think about your own teachers. Without naming anyone, describe what you think makes a good teacher.

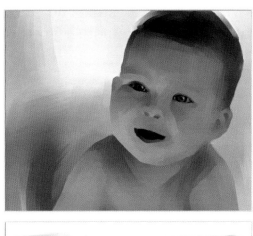

▲ *The 4 seasons can be compared to the 4 stages in human life*

Seeds are sown, the rain falls, the sun shines, the seeds sprout, the plants grow. It happens every year. If anything goes wrong, people will not have enough food.

Long ago, people made up festivals to make sure nothing went wrong. At the beginning of spring, they prayed that the plants would grow. At harvest time, in the autumn, they gave thanks.

Most religions still have festivals to do with the seasons. Jews celebrate:
- Passover in the spring
- Shavuot in the summer
- Sukkot in the autumn
- Hanukkah in the winter.

> Everything that happens in this world happens at the time God chooses. The time for planting and the time for pulling up.
>
> *Ecclesiastes 3 verses 1–2*

1 Talk about the 4 stages of life. How is birth like spring, adulthood like summer, growing old like autumn and death like winter?

2 What is your favourite season. Why?

● Passover

▲ *A family celebrates Passover*

Jewish families prepare for Passover by spring-cleaning the house. They want to have a fresh start for this important 8-day festival. It used to be their new year festival. Everything is fresh and new in the spring.

Passover celebrates the Exodus, when the Jews escaped from Egypt. There were 10 plagues before Pharaoh finally let the Jewish slaves go. When the final plague came, the story says that the angel of death PASSED OVER the Jewish houses. This is where the name Passover comes from.

The festival starts with a very special meal. The food is used to tell the story of the Exodus. In the photo, you can see that the family has books so that everyone can follow the story and join in.

A Jewish woman describes part of the evening:

> We have a song which tells about all the things that God did for us when we came out of Egypt. After each verse the children shout 'Dayanu'. It means 'it would have been enough.' If he'd just taken us out of Egypt – if he'd just opened the Red Sea – if he'd just given us food to eat – it would have been enough!

The evening is a mixture of sadness and joy. The Jews do not forget that they were once slaves. And they are sorry for the Egyptians who drowned in the Red Sea. But they celebrate their freedom. After the story of the Exodus, there is eating and singing late into the night. Another Jewish woman tells us more about it:

> We always have friends and relatives, or people we don't even know. We invite strangers, people who don't have anywhere to go, so that every Jew can celebrate the Passover.

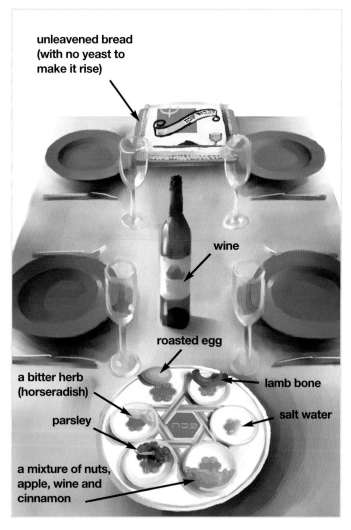

unleavened bread (with no yeast to make it rise)

wine

roasted egg

a bitter herb (horseradish)

lamb bone

parsley

salt water

a mixture of nuts, apple, wine and cinnamon

▲ *These special foods are used to tell the Passover story*

40

A Festival of Light – Hanukkah

▲ *Children love Hanukkah. This photo shows the last and best day of the festival*

Hanukkah brings light to the dark winter months. Light speaks to Jews of hope and the presence of God.

Hanukkah celebrates an event which happened over 2000 years ago. The Jews had been conquered. They were not allowed to worship God. They were put to death if they read the Torah. After years of fighting, a group of Jews defeated the invaders and drove them out of Jerusalem. They cleaned up the Temple and dedicated it once more for the worship of the One God. Hanukkah means 'dedication'.

One of the first things they did was to light the big 7-branched candlestick in the Temple. There was only enough oil for one night, and it would take 8 days to get more. They lit it anyway. It remained burning for 8 days! This is why Hanukkah is an 8-day festival.

At Hanukkah, Jews have a special candlestick which they put in their windows. It has places for 8 candles (as well as a 'servant candle' to light the others). One candle is lit on the first evening, 2 on the second, and so on. Families celebrate Hanukkah with songs, presents and parties.

1 Light is important in many rituals – religious and non-religious. For example, we light candles on birthday cakes.
Why do you think light is used in these rituals?

2 Draw a Hanukkah candlestick. In each of the 8 flames, write about something that you hope for in life.

3 Talk about something that your family celebrates every year. (It does not have to be religious.)

43

● Rosh Hashanah and Yom Kippur

Rosh Hashanah is the Jewish New Year. It celebrates the creation of the world. The Jewish year 5761 began in our year 2000. New Year is a time for looking back and looking forward.

> We look back and ask ourselves 'Have we really done what we meant to do?' If we find that we haven't, we should feel guilty and think 'Never again! Next year we'll be better.'
>
> *Lord Jakobovits*

There is a special New Year meal. The family dip their first piece of bread in honey and say 'May God give me a sweet and happy New Year!' They have apples dipped in honey, too. Many families send Rosh Hashanah cards. You may see them in card shops in early autumn.

Jews believe that God keeps a Book of Life. It has the names of those whom God has forgiven. God decides this on the first day of each year. But anyone who is left out has 10 days to show that they are sorry. During that time, Jews try to say sorry to everyone they have been unkind to during the year.

Yom Kippur comes at the end of the 10 days. It means Day of Atonement. 'Atonement' means to make up for things you have done wrong. This is the day when Jews say sorry to God, and ask for his forgiveness.

Synagogues are packed for Rosh Hashanah and Yom Kippur. They are called High Holydays because they are so important.

This message was sent by Lord Jacobovits when he was the British Chief Rabbi:

> I wish my fellow Jews and, through them, my fellow men, 'Shana Tovah', a good New Year. May we contribute to the wonderful world into which we were created.

▲ *A shofar is blown at Rosh Hashanah. It is a ram's horn*

How do you think you would feel if you were here? You have written down something you have done wrong and feel bad about. Then you see the bit of paper go up in smoke!

Jews go without food during Yom Kippur, to show that they are really sorry for what they have done wrong. Yom Kippur starts with an evening service in the synagogue. This is one of the most important services of the year, and the synagogue is full of people. There are also services throughout the day. Yom Kippur ends with a single blast of the shofar. After that Jews can eat again. The past is now behind them and they have a fresh start in life.

Jews have special rituals to say sorry and be forgiven. This is important for everyone, not just for religious believers. Everyone has to come to terms with things they do wrong. There are times when everyone needs a fresh start. The picture shows what one group of people might do.

New Year

1 New Year is a time for looking back and looking forward.
Think back over the last 12 months:
- What things are you thankful for?
- What things are you sorry for?
Think about the next 12 months:
- What would you like to achieve in that time?

Forgiveness

2 Do you think it is a good idea to try to remember things you have done wrong? Give your reasons.

3 In groups, make up a ceremony of forgiveness.
- Who would take part?
- What will they do to say sorry?
- How would you show they had been forgiven?

● Purim

Purim comes in February or March. It is fun for both children and adults. But the theme of Purim is serious. It is the message that God saved the Jews from being wiped out.

The story of Purim is told in the Book of Esther in the Bible. It happened about 2500 years ago. Esther was a beautiful young woman who was married to the King of Persia. But he didn't know that she was Jewish. The prime minister, Haman, hated the Jews and plotted to kill them. He drew lots to decide when to do it. Purim means 'lots'. Anyone who went to the king without permission was put to death. But Esther dared to go and tell her husband. The king forgave her for breaking the law, and Haman was put to death.

At Purim, Jews read out this story in the synagogue. Every time Haman's name is read, people stamp their feet and boo and hiss. It is just like a pantomime. After synagogue, children have fancy dress parties. Some visit Jewish houses to collect money for charity. They may sing this song:

▲ *These Purim cakes are called 'Haman's Ears'!*

> Today is Purim, tomorrow no more.
> Give me a penny.
> I'll be gone from your door.

Key words	
shofar	**Rosh Hashanah**
Yom Kippur	**Purim**

▲ *Children in fancy-dress for Purim*

1 Draw a picture-strip to tell the story of Esther.

2 The theme of Purim is still important today. What did Hitler do to the Jews in the 20th century (see pages 52–54)?

46

> The world exists only through the breath of schoolchildren.
>
> *The Talmud*

▲ *The future of Judaism depends on children like these*

Jewish teachings claim that 'the world exists *only* through the breath of schoolchildren.' This is because young people are the future. *You* will carry on when the older generation has passed away.

But the past is important too. Without your parents, you wouldn't be here. And if older people did not teach you how to use computers, or how to play tennis, those skills would die out. The future generations depend on the past.

Jewish children learn about Judaism from their parents and teachers. If they did not, their religion and way of life would die out. There are still Jews today, thousands of years after Abraham. The reason for this is that adults have shown their children how to follow Judaism.

47

1 Think about the future, and imagine you have children of your own.
- In what ways would you like family life to be much the same as now?
- In what ways do you think life will be different for your children?

2 List FIVE things you are thankful for from the past.

3 What new skills do you have that your parents do not have?

The Torah tells parents to teach their children. Young Jews are taught many customs and religious rules They learn what foods to eat and what clothes to wear at certain times. By celebrating Jewish festivals, they learn about important events in their history. They learn to read the Hebrew Bible.

Karen and Rosalind are Orthodox Jews. Their children are aged between 3 and 12. One of Karen's favourite verses in the Torah is: 'You shall teach the commandments to your children.' Rosalind gave this reason for wanting her children to learn about Judaism:

> The children must be educated to understand Judaism. Then they can at least choose with knowledge. They can marry Jews or not. They can be Orthodox or not. But they will know what they are taking on.

Jewish children learn a lot at home. But they can also go to religion school. This often takes place at the synagogue on Sunday afternoons. Some young people go until they are 19. They take exams in Jewish Studies. They can also teach the younger children Bible stories and the Hebrew alphabet.

But it's not all hard work! There are Jewish youth clubs too. They can also go on camps to meet other young Jews. This is what one teenage girl said:

> The camps are great fun. They have themes like Israel, and Jews around the world. I have been attending camps since I was 7. Every year I enjoy them more and more.

Her youth group also goes to camps in Israel. One of the aims of these camps is to encourage young Jews to come and live in Israel. The summer camps give them a chance to find out what it is like there.

1 a) Write a sentence to describe how Jewish children learn about Judaism.

b) Give TWO reasons why it is important that they do this.

c) What reason does Rosalind give?

d) Do you think this is a good reason? Talk about it with a partner.

2 Young Jews may meet each other on youth camps. Where do you meet young people who have the same interests as you?

▲ *A Jewish youth camp*

Jews have lived in Britain for over 300 years. There are only about 300,000 here now. Most of them live together in the big cities like London and Manchester. Three of them tell us what it is like:

- We nearly all drive and use electricity on Saturday. We send our children to English state schools. We eat non-kosher meat, bread and milk. And yet we remain a Jewish community. We get together for festival services and parties.

- It is difficult to buy kosher food in country areas. Also most shops are open on Saturdays (our Sabbath) and closed on Sundays (our weekday).
  Our children are different in school, from as early as 5 years old. This can be very upsetting, especially at Christmas time.

Most Jews mix freely with non-Jews at work or school or where they live. But they still feel strongly about their Jewishness. An Orthodox Jewish teenager explains:

I do not think that being Jewish affects my friendships because most of my friends are non-Jewish. But I would not get into a serious relationship with a non-Jewish boy and I shall definitely marry a Jew.

- As a Jew, I have found no problems. Many Jews take part in non-Jewish society while keeping their Jewishness. Many of us talk to groups about Judaism and invite friends to share in Jewish festivals and services.

▶ *A famous Jewish restaurant in London . . . it is not so easy to buy kosher food outside the big cities.*

Members of this synagogue help both Jews and non-Jews:

> We support a local Jewish home for children with learning difficulties. Many of us are 'aunties and uncles'. We take the children home for tea, or take them out for the afternoon.
>
> We also help at the local hospital. But that's not just for Jews. It's organised by the Red Cross.

▲ *Jews who live together in cities find it easier to keep their Jewishness*

The Council of Christians and Jews was founded in Britain in 1942. Its main aim is for Christians and Jews to understand each other's religions. It is trying to break down barriers between them. There are signs that this is working:

> In recent years, I have come across non-Jewish groups who have wanted to understand the Jewish religion. Many people at my synagogue have a strong wish to understand other minority religions. They also want to be understood themselves.

The Archbishop of Canterbury called for Christians and Jews to act together. This was his reason:

> Our shared belief in One God calls us to speak together, again and again, in the modern world.

1 Using page 49:
   a) Give THREE examples of how Jews mix with other people in Britain today.

   b) Give TWO examples of how they keep their Jewishness.

2 a) How can it be difficult for Jews in non-Jewish countries to keep all their own rules?
   b) Why is it easier for Jews living in big cities, than in county areas?
3 Describe ONE way in which Jews help others.

● Lord Immanuel Jakobovits

In October 1999, about 3000 people gathered for a service in memory of Lord Immanuel Jakobovits.   He had been the chief rabbi of Jews in the UK from 1967 to 1991.   He was 78 when he died.

He came to Britain from Germany in the 1930s when he was 13 years old.   He escaped from the persecution of the Jews by Hitler.   He was welcomed in this country.

When he grew up, he became the friend of many political and religious leaders.   He was a personal friend of Margaret Thatcher when she was Prime Minister in the 1980s. At the time of his death, the Prime Minister, Tony Blair, said this:

> Lord Jakobovits was a man deeply respected and widely admired through the whole of the country for his faith, his ability and his courage.

Lord Jakobovits was an Orthodox Jew, but he wanted all kinds of Jews to get on well together.   He held secret talks between the different groups who did not get on. He knew that 6 million Jews had been killed under Hitler's rule, and he thought that Jews should stand by each other against their enemies.   He also worked hard to improve relations between Jews and Christians.

▲ *Lord Jakobovits*

1 Imagine you were Immanuel Jakobovits arriving in this country at the age of 13. What do you think he would have found strange?

2 Tony Blair spoke of THREE things that people in this country liked about Lord Jakobovits. What were the THREE things?

So long as you can feel
the cold –
the wet –
the hunger,
and the lice –
which itch,
and drink your blood
You are alive –
Rejoice
You will survive
Be strong,
it can't be long.

> *Michael Etkind, a survivor of the Holocaust*

In 70 CE (Common Era), the Romans attacked the Holy City of Jerusalem. This was the centre of the Jewish Promised Land. They destroyed the Temple. Thousands of Jews were killed. Many were taken as slaves.

It's hard to understand what the loss of the Temple meant to those Jews of old. It was so much more than just blocks of stone to them. They believed with all their hearts that God lived in the Temple. They believed that when it was destroyed his presence left it.

> *Lynne Reid Banks,*
> Letters to my Israeli Sons, (adapted)

The Temple has never been rebuilt. All that remains of it is the Western Wall that holds up the mount on which the Temple stood. People call it the Wailing Wall. This is because Jews still come here and feel sad about the Temple.

After their defeat by the Romans, the Jews were thrown out of Israel. They lived in countries all over the Middle East and Europe.

▲ *A Jew prays at the Western Wall*

Jews in non-Jewish countries were often feared and hated. This was just because they were different.

▲ *Jews in the Middle Ages sometimes had to wear special clothes to make them look different*

One of the most terrible examples of this hatred took place in Europe in the middle of the 20th century. It was caused by Hitler, the ruler of Germany. He believed that Jews were less than human, and he tried to wipe them out.

52

Anne Frank is a famous Jewish teenager from this time. She lived in Amsterdam in Holland. She wrote a diary for 3 years. At first, it is the kind of thing any teenage girl would write today. But then the Nazis invaded Holland in 1940. They made new laws which made life very difficult for the Jews. Anne tells us what life was like:

> Jews must wear a yellow star, Jews must hand in their bicycles, Jews are banned from trams and are forbidden to drive. Jews are forbidden to visit theatres, cinemas, and other places of entertainment. Swimming baths, tennis courts and other sports grounds are all closed to them. Jews may not visit Christians.

▲ *Anne Frank*

By October 1942, Anne wrote that things had got worse:

> Our many Jewish friends are being taken away. These people are treated by the Gestapo without a shred of decency. They are loaded into cattle trucks and sent to concentration camps . . . We assume that most of them are being murdered. The British radio speaks of them being gassed.

In 1942 Hitler began rounding up the Jews. For two long years, Anne lived in hiding with her family. (You can still visit this house in Amsterdam.) In all that time, she did not give up hope:

> In spite of everything I still believe that people are really good at heart. If I look up into the heavens, I think that it will all come right. Peace will return again.

Her family was found out and taken to a concentration camp. She died from disease just a month before the war ended. She was 15. Her father was the only one to live through the war. He kept his daughter's diary. Later, this was published and became a best-seller.

The Jews were taken to concentration camps. The strongest had to work like slaves. Many died from disease and starvation. Most were gassed or shot dead, and their bodies burned. 12,000,000 people died in this way. Half of them were Jews. **This mass murder is called the Holocaust.**

At Dachau in Germany, one of these camps is now a museum. On the wall is written in French, English, German and Russian:

NEVER AGAIN

Many people, not only Jews, want young people to learn about what happened. They hope this will stop anything like this happening again.

Karen, an Orthodox Jewess, goes into schools to talk about Judaism:

> One day, perhaps one of those children I talk to, will meet someone who doesn't do things quite the way *they* do things. Who maybe won't eat the same food as they eat, or has their head covered. And perhaps they will understand why, and accept it. And it just might make the world a little easier to live in.

◀ *1995 – Jews remember the dead at a concentration camp in Poland*

1 Imagine you were a Jew when the Temple was destroyed. Write down SIX different words to describe your feelings.

2 Draw FOUR things that the Jews were not allowed to do under Hitler.

3 a) Do you think we should remember the Holocaust? Give your reasons.

b) What could be done in this country to help people remember it? (Think of different kinds of memorials.)

Thousands of Jews lost their homes in the Second World War. Afterwards, many countries agreed that they should have a land of their own. So, **2000 years after they were thrown out by the Romans, Israel became once more a Jewish country**. One Jewish man who was living there in a Jewish community said this:

> It was during the night. We were asleep and everybody was listening to the radio. When the news came, they woke us up and brought us to the dining-hall. Everybody was dancing. We were in our pyjamas and on our parents' shoulders.

But not everyone accepted the new State of Israel. Arabs had lived there for the past 2000 years. They did not want to see it given to the Jews. Since 1948 there have been a number of wars between Israel and the Arab countries around Israel.

In the Six Day War of June 1967, the Israelis conquered the part of Jerusalem that had been given to the Arabs in 1948. One Jewish soldier remembers it well:

> And so it was that on the morning of 7 June 1967, I stood for the first time at the Western Wall. At Judaism's most sacred place. And I, who am not a practising Jew, covered my head and wept – as all the Jews back to Abraham would have done.

star of David

stripes of tallit

▲ *Jerusalem today is a mix of old and new. It is also a centre for 3 religions: Judaism, Christianity and Islam*

◀ *The flag of Israel*

The problem of Jews and Arabs in Israel is still not solved.   Some fighting still goes on.   The photo above shows Yitzhak Rabin (left), who was then Prime Minister of Israel shaking hands with Yasser Arafat (right), the head of the PLO (Palestinian Liberation Organisation).   The 2 leaders agreed to work for peace.   Sadly, a Jew shot dead Mr Rabin shortly after this.

The Arab and Jewish leaders are still struggling for peace.   Much hard feeling and years of bloodshed lie behind this struggle.   Jews and Arabs have been cruel to each other.   Both sides have dropped bombs and gunned people down.   Memories go back a long way.

▶ *Some people don't want to give up anything for peace (like the Jew who shot Rabin).   But there are others, on both sides, who want peace. The people in the photo are both Jews and Arabs*

Jews have different views about the land of Israel:

> Israel was given by God to the Jewish people.   I believe in the biblical borders of the State of Israel.
>
> *Malvyn Benjamin, Orthodox*
>
> I agree that Israel is a God-given land.   But my religious beliefs do not include an idea of borders as being more important than peace.
>
> *Charles Emmanuel, Reform*

The Jews will not give up their Promised Land.   But they want their children to be able to grow up there in peace.   An Orthodox Jewish girl explains:

> The State of Israel is so very important because it is the true home of the Jews.
>
> Being Jewish is not just a religion.   It is also a nationality.
>
> After all our forefathers have been through to keep our homeland, I think every Jew should go and live there.   I am returning once I am 18.

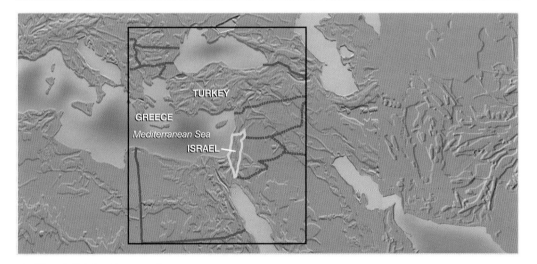

▲ *The Middle East today*

1 Copy the flag of Israel on page 55 into your books.   Notice the Jewish symbols it has on it.

2 Jews call Israel 'The Promised Land'.   Who do they think promised it to them?

3 Give ONE reason why Jews and Arabs have fought over Israel.

4 One of the photos on page 56 shows people with banners saying 'Peace Now'.   What symbol of peace could you draw on a banner instead of writing words?

5 You can only end a quarrel if both sides want to, and if both sides are prepared to give something up.   In groups, make up a role-play on this idea.   You will need to decide on the characters – what they quarrel about – and what they do to make up.

TASK

Talk about:
- difficulties people might have who go to live in another country;
- ways in which you could help a new pupil who has come from another country.

There are about 14 million Jews today. Less than 6 million live in Israel. The others live in many different countries. Many live in the USA, particularly New York.

Jews are law-abiding citizens, and in most countries they are free to get on with their lives. They can meet in synagogues, hold festivals and study the Torah.

However, this is not true everywhere. In the old days of the Soviet Union, for example, life was very difficult for them. Many synagogues were closed and very few Jewish books were on sale.

Jews came from all over the Soviet Union when there was an Israeli stand at the 1987 Moscow Book Fair. They wanted to see the books about Judaism and Israel. It was also a chance to talk to other Jews. This is what one Israeli said:

I will never forget a 14-year-old boy who had travelled 1000 miles by train to get here. He had queued for 5 hours and then had less than an hour to look at the books and talk to the Israelis. He set off on his journey home clutching a star of David we gave him.

Many Russian Jews wanted to live in Israel or the USA. They had to be given permission to leave Russia. If the government refused to let them go, these Jews were called Refuseniks. One man waited 20 years before he was allowed to go.

People in other countries used to write letters to the Soviet Union and hold protests. Now that the Union is in smaller states, Jews have more freedom.

▶ *A Jew in a synagogue in North Africa*

Ida Nudel was a Refusenik for 16 years, waiting to join her sister in Israel. There is a happy ending to the story. Ida was finally allowed to leave Russia. She said this to her supporters:

> I thank people of goodwill the world over. From Presidents and Prime Ministers to people from all walks of life. I want to thank all of you who spoke up for me. During all those years, I felt the sympathy of thousands of people, Jews and non-Jews alike.

Some Jews in Russia were imprisoned for criticising the government. Nathan Sharansky was in jail for 9 years. His wife gave him a book of the Psalms. This is what it meant to him:

> This book helped me to feel a link with my wife, with my people, my history, with God. It helped me to feel that I was together with my wife and with my people during all those years.

▼ *A protest to let Jews go free*

1 You have thought about difficulties people might have when they go to live in another country. What difficulties might Jews have in particular?

2 One Jewish Refusenik waited 16 years before being allowed to leave Russia. During that time people kept up pressure on the government.

a) Have you ever joined a protest? Talk about what it was and if it achieved its purpose.

b) What do you feel strongly about? Make a class list.

c) Choose ONE thing that you feel strongly about. What can you do about it?

d) Can you think of anything that is so important that you would wait 16 years for it?

> The Law of Moses has changed people who come into contact with it, even though they seem to have cast the Law aside.
>
> *A 12th-century Jew*

Judaism is only a small religion, but it has influenced many people's lives. It has certainly influenced Christianity.

Jesus himself was a Jew. The Ten Commandments are as important to Christians as to Jews. The Jewish Bible has been taken by Christians into their own Bible. They call it the Old Testament. The stories of Noah's Ark, Jonah and the Whale, Daniel in the Lion's Den, are all from this part of the Bible. There is a reading from the Old Testament in church services. Psalms are sung which were made up by the Jewish King David. Christian Holy Communion comes from the Jewish custom of sharing bread and wine at special meals.

There are close links between the 3 religions: Judaism, Christianity and Islam. They all believe in the One God. They all teach their followers to be good people, because God is good. There is a reason why so many things are the same. All 3 religions can trace their beginnings back to Abraham, as the diagram shows.

Flora Solomon lives in a flat in London. She is Jewish. Many of her neighbours are Arabs (who are Muslims):

> I met one in the lift the other day and I said 'I am a Jew and you are an Arab.' And he said, 'Madame, we are cousins.' And he kissed my hand!

A rabbi tells us of 2 important gifts the Jews have given us:

> Everybody knows that a week is 7 days. The Lord rested from His creation on the 7th day. No other people had the idea of having a 7-day week. That's one of the gifts of Judaism to the world.
>
> Another gift is the law of charity to the poor. You may not neglect any suffering. Let me take one example that made a deep impression on me as a child. If you see your neighbour's horse or donkey lying collapsed in the street, you may not ignore it. You must help that animal and your neighbour.

Rabbi Julia Neuberger sums up what she thinks is Judaism's main message to its followers and to the world:

> I think we have a duty to do God's will. To me, a lot of it is being concerned for the wider community. We should be concerned for the underprivileged, the prisoners, the poor. That's the great message of Judaism.

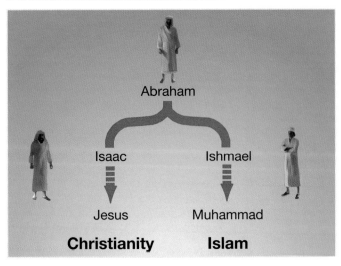

▲ *Abraham's family tree*

Jews, Christians and Muslims have much in common.   But sadly they have not always lived in peace together.   Today, many followers of all 3 religions are trying to live in peace with each other. If great religions cannot live in peace, what hope is there for the nations of the world?

This statue stands in the grounds of Yad Vashem.   This is a place of memorial to the 6 million Jews killed in the Holocaust.   It reminds the world of the evil of racism. Races, religions and cultures can be very different from each other. But they need not be a threat to each other.   The Jews remind us that we all have rights and that we all have our own special ways.

◀ *You can almost hear the cry from this statue, as a parent holds in its arms a dead child.   It stands for all Jewish parents who lost their children in the Holocaust.   It stands for Israel as she weeps for all the Jews who have been killed*

1 What are the TWO main beliefs that link Judaism, Christianity and Islam?

2 Find TWO things on page 60 that Judaism has given to the world.

3 A Jew tells of helping his neighbour's horse or donkey.   Talk about ways in which we can help our neighbours today.

Glossary

Abraham – the Father of the Jews
ambassador – someone who represents another country
ancient – very old
Ark – cupboard in which the Torah scrolls are kept

Bar Mitzvah – Son of the Commandment, Jewish boy's coming of age
Bat Mitzvah – Daughter of the Commandment, Jewish girl's coming of age
Bible – holy book of the Jews (and Christians)

challah – rich bread for the Sabbath
circumcision – the loose skin of the penis is cut off
commandment – order (from God)
community – group of people
concentration camp – camp where people are forced to stay
congregation – group of people who worship together
cremation – the burning of a corpse to ashes
culture – way of life

Exodus – the escape of the Jews from Egypt – a book in the Bible

famine – lack of food

Hanukkah – Jewish festival of lights
Hebrew – Jewish language
holocaust – total destruction
Holocaust – mass murder caused by Hitler

Jewess – female Jew

kosher – fit for use according to Jewish laws

logo – sign

menorah – 7–branched candlestick
Messiah – promised Saviour of the Jews
mezuzah – small box for the Shema, fixed to door frame
minorities – small groups of people

Orthodox – traditional Judaism

parchment – animal skin used for writing on
Passover – Jewish festival to celebrate the Exodus
Pharaoh – ruler of ancient Egypt
plague – a disaster that strikes an area
Promised Land – land promised in the Bible by God to the Jews
prophet – someone who speaks God's words
proverb – wise saying
psalm – religious poem put to music
Purim – festival of lots

quill – a pen made from a large feather

rabbi – Jewish teacher
Reform – modern Judaism
Refuseniks – Russians not allowed to leave Russia
ritual – repeated words or actions in religion
Rosh Hashanah – Jewish New Year

Sabbath – Jewish holy day/day of rest
sacrifice – offering to God
scribe – writer
scroll – book in the form of rolled up paper
sermon – religious talk given by minister
Shabbat – Sabbath day
Shema – statement of Jewish beliefs
shofar – ram's horn
spiritual – to do with a person's inner spirit
sukkah – hut
Sukkot – name of autumn harvest festival
symbol – something that stands for something else
synagogue – Jewish place of worship

Tenach – name for Jewish Bible
Torah – first 5 books of Bible

volunteers – people who do things without pay

Yad Vashem – memorial place in Israel for the Holocaust
Yom Kippur – Day of Atonement

Index